THE WORLD'S SMALLEST ANIMALS

THE WORLD'S SMALLEST INSECTS

by Becca Becker

pogo

Ideas for Parents and Teachers

Pogo Books let children practice reading informational text while introducing them to nonfiction features such as headings, labels, sidebars, maps, and diagrams, as well as a table of contents, glossary, and index.

Carefully leveled text with a strong photo match offers early fluent readers the support they need to succeed.

Before Reading

- "Walk" through the book and point out the various nonfiction features. Ask the student what purpose each feature serves.
- Look at the glossary together. Read and discuss the words.

Read the Book

- Have the child read the book independently.
- Invite him or her to list questions that arise from reading.

After Reading

- Discuss the child's questions. Talk about how he or she might find answers to those questions.
- Prompt the child to think more. Ask: What small insects have you seen? What did they look like?

Pogo Books are published by Jump!
5357 Penn Avenue South
Minneapolis, MN 55419
www.jumplibrary.com

Library of Congress Cataloging-in-Publication Data

Names: Becker, Becca, author.
Title: The world's smallest insects / by Becca Becker.
Description: Minneapolis, MN: Jump!, Inc., [2025]
Series: The world's smallest animals | Includes index.
Audience: Ages 7-10
Identifiers: LCCN 2023057565 (print)
LCCN 2023057566 (ebook)
ISBN 9798892131940 (hardcover)
ISBN 9798892131957 (paperback)
ISBN 9798892131964 (ebook)
Subjects: LCSH: Insects—Juvenile literature | Insects—Size—Juvenile literature. | Body size—Juvenile literature.
Classification: LCC QL467.2 .B4268 2025 (print)
LCC QL467.2 (ebook)
DDC 595.7—dc23/eng/20240123
LC record available at https://lccn.loc.gov/2023057565
LC ebook record available at https://lccn.loc.gov/2023057566

Editor: Alyssa Sorenson
Designer: Molly Ballanger

Photo Credits: Alexan2008/iStock, cover; chinahbzyg/Shutterstock, 1; Kletr/Shutterstock, 3; Potapov Alexander/Shutterstock, 4 (left); Ken Griffiths/Shutterstock, 4 (right); SewCreamStudio/Shutterstock, 5; Gary Webber/Dreamstime, 6-7; topimages/Shutterstock, 8 (left), 22 (dragonfly); Africa Studio/Shutterstock, 8 (right); Lewis Tse/Shutterstock, 9; milehightraveler/iStock, 10-11, 22 (butterfly); Shannon Foreman/iNaturalist, 12, 22 (mosquito); pryzmat/Shutterstock, 12-13; Fabio Sacchi/Shutterstock, 14-15 (ant); Brian V. Brown/Wikimedia, 14-15 (fly), 22 (fly); PeopleImages/iStock, 16-17 (scientist); John T. Huber, 16-17 (wasp), 22 (*Kikiki huna*); Katja Schulz/Flickr, 18-19; The Natural History Museum, London/Science Source, 19, 22 (*Dicopomorpha echmepterygis*); Robb Hannawacker/Flickr, 20; Belizar/Dreamstime, 21; Dreamframer/Shutterstock, 23.

Printed in the United States of America at Corporate Graphics in North Mankato, Minnesota.

TABLE OF CONTENTS

CHAPTER 1
Crawling and Flying 4

CHAPTER 2
Tiny Bugs 8

CHAPTER 3
Important Insects 20

ACTIVITIES & TOOLS
How Small? 22
Try This! 23
Glossary 23
Index 24
To Learn More 24

CHAPTER 1

CRAWLING AND FLYING

A bee lands on a flower. An ant carries a leaf. These animals look and act different, but they are both insects.

There are more than 1 million insect **species**. About 7,000 new ones are discovered every year! They live all around the world.

All insects have two **antennas**. They have six legs. They have **exoskeletons**. Many have wings.

Some insects are big, like the giant weta. Others are small. Let's learn about the smallest!

TAKE A LOOK!

An insect has three main body parts. What are they and the other parts called? Take a look!

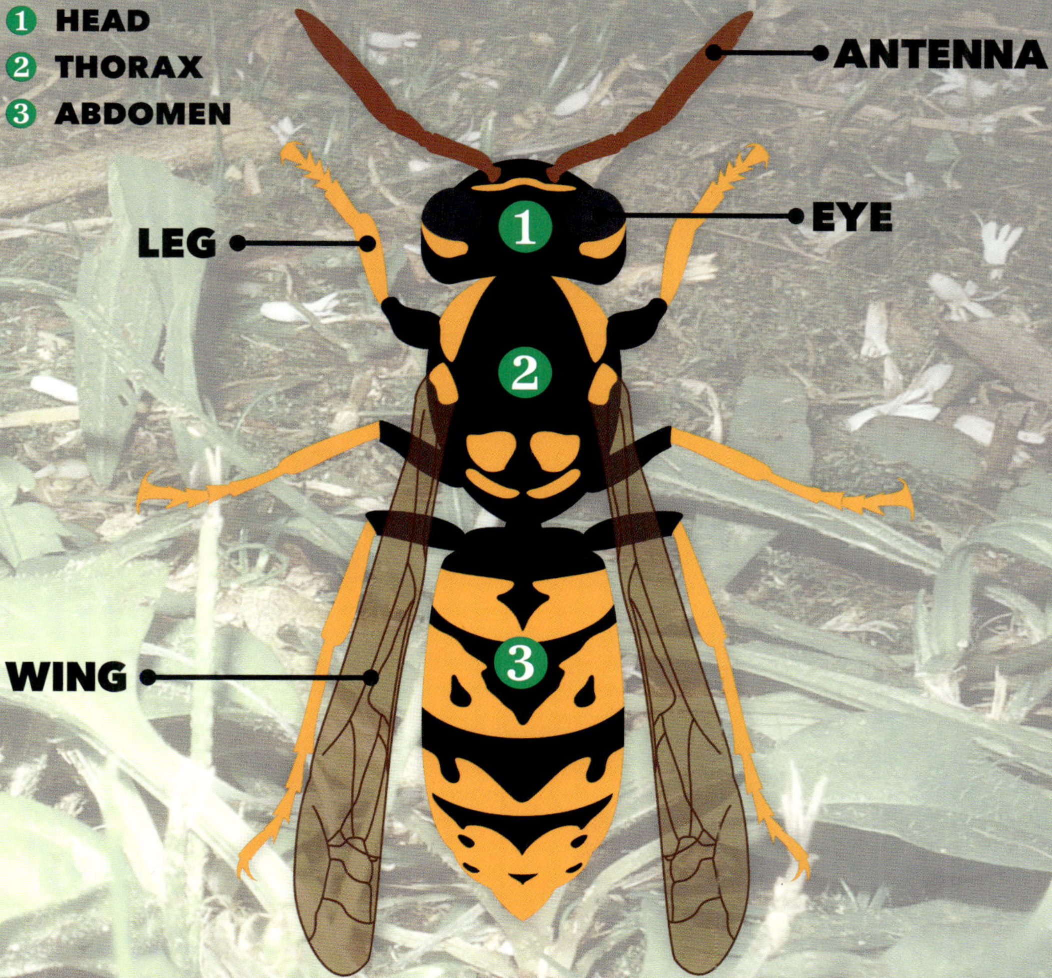

CHAPTER 2

TINY BUGS

The scarlet dwarf is the smallest dragonfly. It lives in China, Japan, and southeast Asia. It lives and flies in the mountains. Its body is shorter than a paper clip!

scarlet dwarf

Length: 0.59 inches (1.5 centimeters)
Wingspan: 0.79 inches (2.0 cm)

It has a short **wingspan**.
It can't fly very far.

western pygmy blue butterfly

Wingspan: 0.47 inches (1.2 cm)

The western pygmy blue is the smallest butterfly. It can fit on your fingernail! It may be tiny, but it travels far. It lives in California, Nevada, New Mexico, and Arizona. But it can go all the way to Arkansas and Louisiana. How? It flies high in the air. The wind carries it.

The smallest mosquito lives in the southern United States. It doesn't bite people. It drinks blood from **amphibians** like frogs.

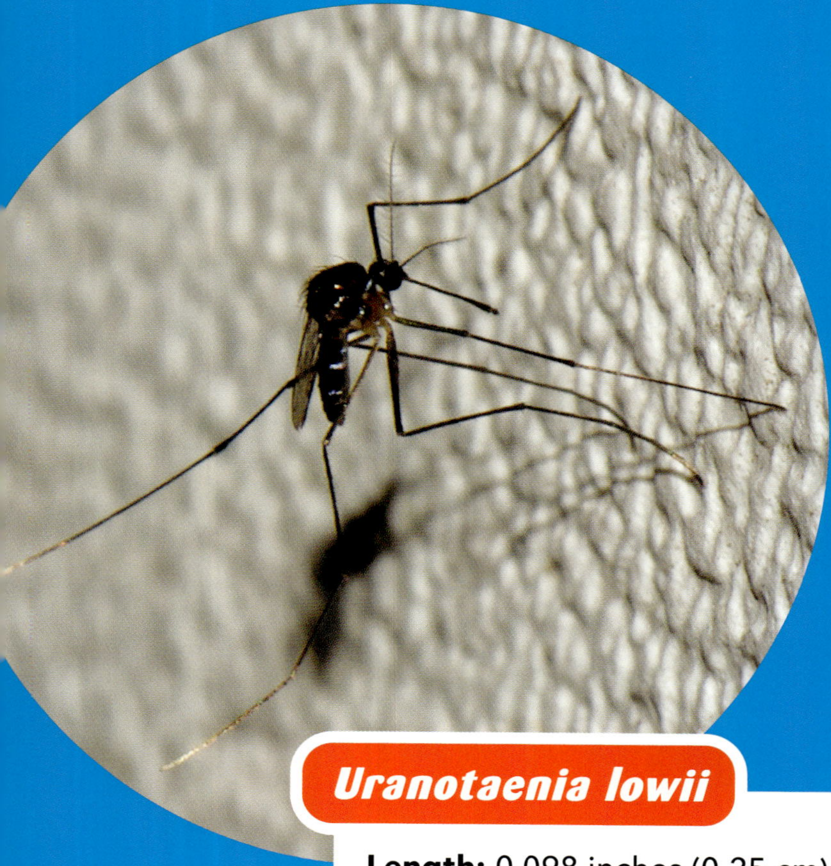

Uranotaenia lowii

Length: 0.098 inches (0.25 cm)

Euryplatea nanaknihali

Length: 0.016 inches (0.04 cm)

The smallest fly is tinier than a dot of pepper! It needs to be small to **survive**. Why? It lays eggs inside an ant's head. When the flies **hatch**, they eat the ant from the inside out.

DID YOU KNOW?

The fly eats tiny ants. These ants are a little longer than a dime is thick!

Kikiki huna is a tiny wasp. It is the smallest flying insect. It is half the size of a grain of salt! You need a **microscope** to see it. Its wings look like **bristles**. Scientists think it is impossible for a bug to get any smaller and still fly.

DID YOU KNOW?

This bug was first found in Hawaii. Its name means "tiny bit."

microscope
Kikiki huna
Length: 0.0059 inches (0.015 cm)

bark louse

A male wasp is the smallest insect we know about. It is tiny for a good reason. It is a **parasite**. It spends most of its life inside a bark louse egg. Why? It eats **nutrients** in the egg.

DID YOU KNOW?

If you lined up 175 of these male wasps, the line would only be 1.0 inch (2.5 cm) long.

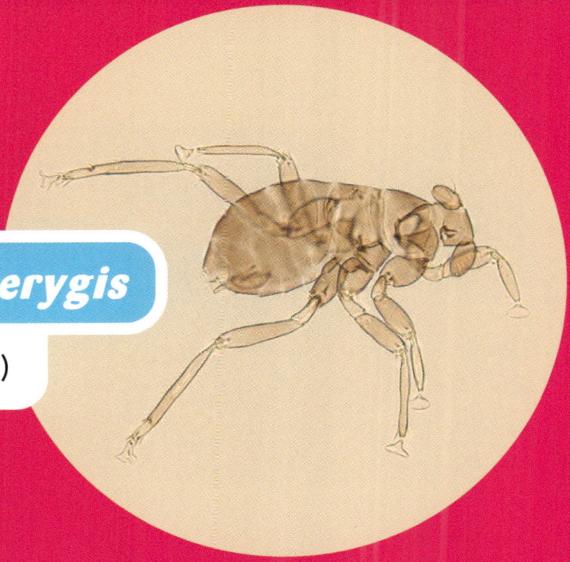

Dicopomorpha echmepterygis

Length: 0.005 inches (0.013 cm)

CHAPTER 3

IMPORTANT INSECTS

Small insects are important to the **environment**. Many are **pollinators**. The western pygmy blue butterfly flies from flower to flower. It spreads pollen. Flowers need this to make seeds.

Small insects are food for larger animals. They are an important part of the **food chain**. Insects keep our environment balanced and healthy!

ACTIVITIES & TOOLS

HOW SMALL?

How small are the smallest insects? How small are they compared to a tack? Take a look!

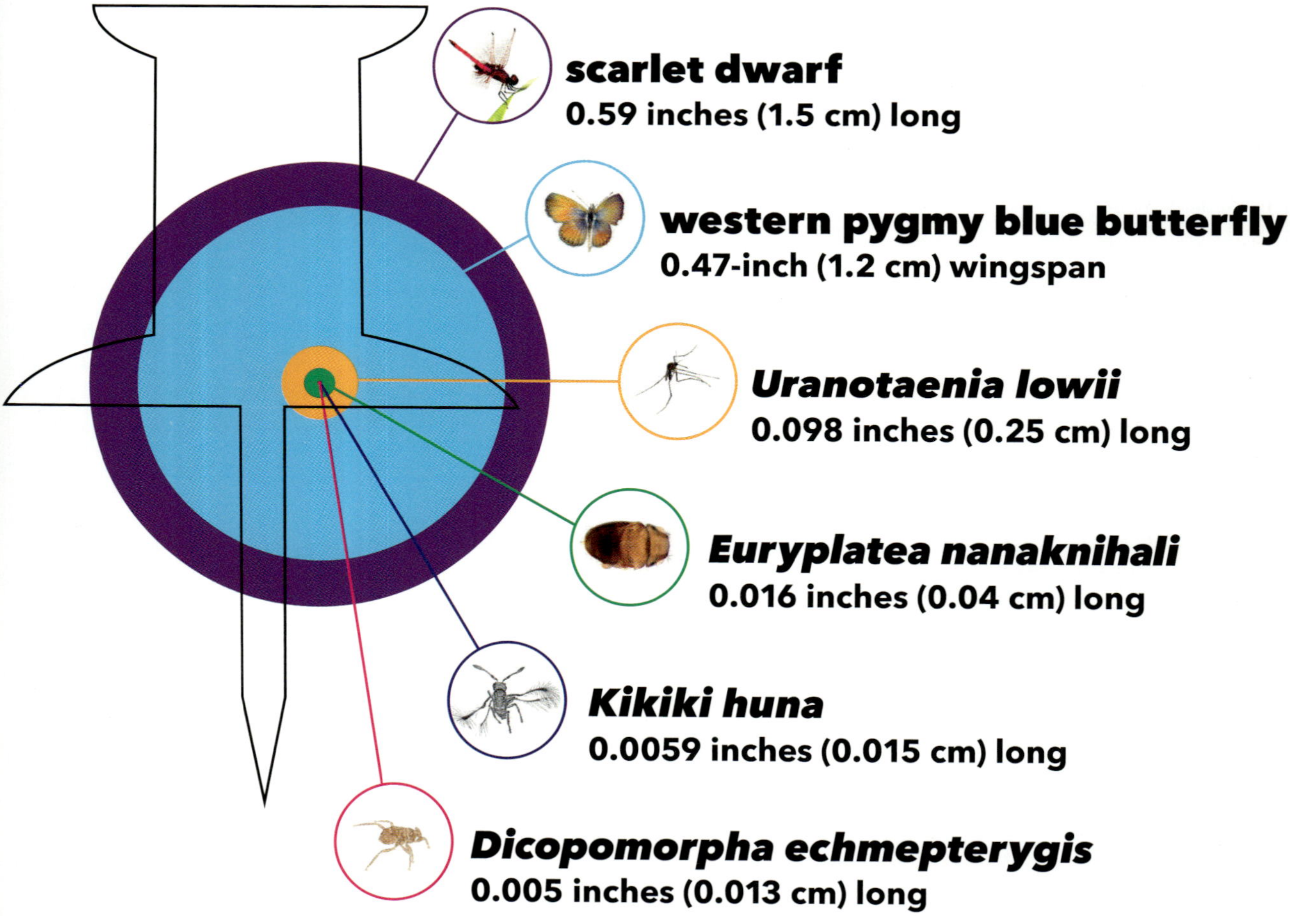

TRY THIS!

Go outside, and find some insects! How small are they? What are they doing? How does their size help them in their environment? Write about your findings.

GLOSSARY

amphibians: Cold-blooded animals with backbones that live in water and on land at different points of their lives.

antennas: Feelers on the head of an insect.

bristles: Short, stiff hairs.

environment: The natural surroundings of living things, such as the air, land, or ocean.

exoskeletons: Hard protective or supporting structures on the outside of insects' bodies.

food chain: An ordered arrangement of animals and plants in which each feeds on the one below it in the chain.

hatch: To break out of an egg.

microscope: An instrument that makes very small things look larger so they can be seen and studied.

nutrients: Substances that animals need to stay strong and healthy.

parasite: An animal that lives and feeds on another animal.

pollinators: Animals that move pollen from one flower to another.

species: One of the groups into which similar animals and plants are divided.

survive: To stay alive.

wingspan: The distance between one end of a wing and the other.

INDEX

ant 4, 15

antennas 6, 7

bee 4

Dicopomorpha echmepterygis 19

eggs 15, 19

environment 20, 21

Euryplatea nanaknihali 14, 15

exoskeletons 6

flower 4, 20

food chain 21

giant weta 6

Kikiki huna 16, 17

microscope 16

nutrients 19

parasite 19

pollinators 20

scarlet dwarf 8, 9

seeds 20

species 5

Uranotaenia lowii 12

western pygmy blue butterfly 10, 11, 20

wingspan 9, 10

TO LEARN MORE

Finding more information is as easy as 1, 2, 3.

1. Go to www.factsurfer.com
2. Enter "world'ssmallestinsects" into the search box.
3. Choose your book to see a list of websites.

FACT SURFER